Verbal Reasoning
Progress Papers 1

Patrick Berry

Schofield & Sims

Introduction

The **Verbal Reasoning Progress Papers** provide structured activities that increase in difficulty throughout the series, developing your knowledge and skills in verbal reasoning. Use the books to prepare for school entrance examinations and to improve your verbal reasoning skills.

How to use this book

There are six papers in this book. Each contains 100 questions, divided by topic into sets of five. A single paper may take between 45 and 75 minutes to complete, and you might need two or more sessions to complete one paper.

- For exam preparation, revision and all-round practice, you may choose to work through the papers in numerical order. Once you have completed a paper, ask a teacher, parent or adult helper to correct any mistakes and to explain where you went wrong.

- To practise a topic that you find particularly challenging, work through selected activities in order of difficulty using the **Topics chart**, available to download from the Schofield & Sims website.

Answers

The answers to all the questions in this book can be found in a pull-out section in the middle. You (or an adult) should use this to mark your work at the end of each paper. You will receive one mark for each correct answer, giving you a total mark out of 100 for every paper. Take time to learn and remember why the answer given is correct.

Use the **Progress chart** at the back of this book to record your marks and measure progress.

Downloads

Free downloads are available from the Schofield & Sims website (www.schofieldandsims.co.uk/free-downloads), including extra practice material.

Published by **Schofield & Sims Ltd,**
7 Mariner Court, Wakefield, West Yorkshire WF4 3FL, UK
Telephone 01484 607080
www.schofieldandsims.co.uk

First published in 2016
This edition copyright © Schofield & Sims Ltd, 2018
Second impression 2018

Author: **Patrick Berry**

Patrick Berry has asserted his moral rights under the Copyright, Designs and Patents Act, 1988, to be identified as the author of this work.

Grateful thanks to Siân Goodspeed and Denise Moulton for their contribution to **Verbal Reasoning Progress Papers**.

British Library Cataloguing in Publication Data
A catalogue record for this book is available from the British Library.

Design by **Oxford Designers and Illustrators Ltd**
Cover design by **Ledgard Jepson Ltd**
Printed in the UK by **Page Bros (Norwich) Ltd**

ISBN 978 07217 1470 7

Contents

Note for parents, tutors, teachers and other adult helpers
A pull-out answers section (pages A1 to A12) appears in the centre of this book, between pages 26 and 27 (Paper 3). This provides answers to all the questions, along with guidance on marking the papers. Remove the pull-out section before the child begins working through the practice papers.

START HERE

Q. 1–5
jumbled words with clues

Each question has a word in <u>CAPITALS</u>. The letters in this word have been mixed up. Use the clue to work out what the word is. Write it on the line.

Example NIBOR (a bird). _ROBIN_

1	MAD	(a beaver builds it)	_Dam_	1
2	STEAKFARB	(a meal)	_Breakfast_	2
3	ROUSTERS	(clothing)	_Trousers_	3
4	LIFES	(insects)	FLIES	4
5	FEARFIG	(an animal)	_Giraffe_	5

Q. 6–10
odd ones out

Two words in each question do **not** belong with the rest. Underline these **two** words.

Example horrid nasty <u>kind</u> mean unfriendly <u>helpful</u>

6	red	green	<u>colour</u>	orange	<u>paint</u>	yellow	6
7	foal	<u>dog</u>	puppy	kitten	<u>cat</u>	calf	7
8	trapezium	<u>triangle</u>	square	rectangle	<u>circle</u>	parallelogram	8
9	<u>bicycle</u>	car	van	lorry	taxi	<u>sledge</u>	9
10	armchair	settee	<u>table</u>	chair	<u>desk</u>	stool	10

Q. 11–15
word grids

Fit each set of words into the grid beside them. The words should read across and down.

11

A	D	O
c	a	n
E	Y	E

one
day
ado
eye
ace
can

12

B	A	T
a	g	o
Y	E	T

tot
ago
bay
yet
bat
age

13

P	A	L
i	r	e
N	E	T

ire
let
pal
net
are
pin

14

N	O	T
a	r	e
P	E	N

nap
ten
ore
not
pen
are

15

S	P	A	R
	e	w	e
S	W	E	D

wed
red
par
ewe
pew
awe

11			
12			
13			
14			
15			

MARK
✓ OR ✗

Q. 16–20	A four-letter word is hidden in each of these sentences. You will find the hidden word at the end of one word and the beginning of the next. Underline the hidden word and then write it on the line.	

spot the word

Example Daniel ended the speech with a joke. ___lend___

16 "I think you were adding up the wrong numbers," Suzy told me. _read_   **16** ✓

17 Esther often goes with her friend to play tennis. _hero_   **17** ✓

18 Max painted the table after he had painted the chairs. ~~tech~~ _leaf_   **18** ✓

19 Theseus said he would go alone to fight the hideous Minotaur. _goal_   **19** ✓

20 Eggs often go bad in very warm weather. _soft_   **20** ✓

Q. 21–25	This is a diagram of a street. The odd house numbers are on one side and the even numbers on the other side. Five children (Adam, Bilal, Claire, David and Ella) live in the street.

position problems

Read the questions and write the answers on the lines. You may write notes on the diagram if this will help you.

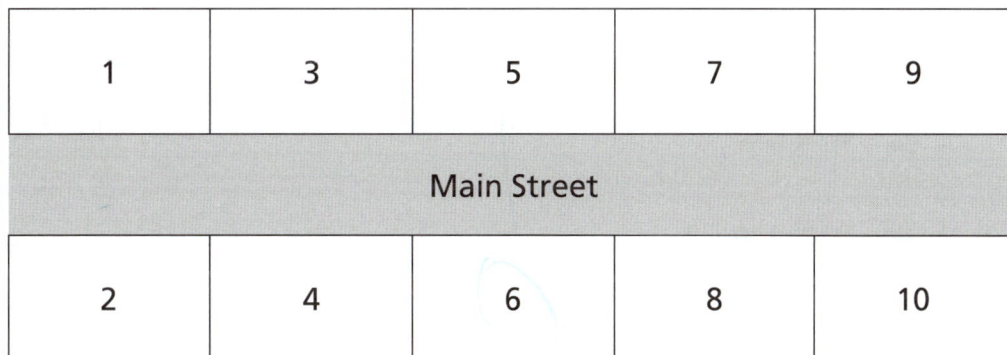

1	3	5	7	9
Main Street				
2	4	6	8	10

21 Adam lives in a house with an even number above 9.
What is the number of Adam's house? _10_   **21** ✓

22 Bilal lives in a house with an odd number that is the square of 3.
What is the number of Bilal's house? _9_   **22** ✓

23 Claire lives next door to Bilal.
What is the number of Claire's house? _7_   **23** ✓

24 David lives in the house two doors along from Adam.
What is the number of David's house? _6_   **24** ✓

25 Ella lives opposite the house that is two to the left of David.
What is the number of Ella's house? _21_   **25**

MARK [ ]

MARK
✓ OR ✗

Q. 26–30

letter codes

Answer these letter analogies. Use the alphabet to help you.

A B C D E F G H I J K L M N O P Q R S T U V W X Y Z

26 A is to B as C is to ___D___ .

27 Z is to Y as F is to ___E___ .

28 D is to G as T is to ___W___ .

29 MN is to OP as FG is to ___HI___ .

30 X is to B as Q is to ___U___ .

26 ✓
27 ✓
28 ✓
29 ✓
30 ✓

Q. 31–35

symbol codes

The word **SHEARED** is written as ▲ ▼ ▶ ◀ ● ▶ ■ in code. Use the same code to work out the hidden words.

31 ▲ ▶ ▶ ■   SEED

32 ■ ◀ ● ▶   DARE

33 ● ▶ ◀ ■   READ

34 ▼ ◀ ● ■   HARD

35 ▶ ◀ ● ▲   EARS

31 ✓
32 ✓
33 ✓
34 ✓
35 ✓

Q. 36–40

missing
three-letter
words

Use the clue to work out the five-letter word. The missing three letters also form a word. Write the three-letter word on the line.

Example S _ _ _ T   (to begin)   _TAR_

36 S _ _ _ K   (to talk)   PEA

37 C _ _ _ E   (a large box)   RAT

38 S _ _ _ K   (a nasty smell)   TIN

39 G _ _ _ N   (got bigger)   ROW

40 P _ _ _ L   (found in an oyster shell)   EAR

36 ✓
37 ☐
38 ✗
39 ✓
40 ✓

MARK ☐

MARK
✓ OR ✗

Q. 41–45

true
statements

Read the information in each question. Circle the **only** statement (A, B, C, D or E) that has to be true, based on this information.

41 Sara is my sister. My name is Dan. We live with our parents.

    A Dad's name is Dan.

    B Dan has no grandpa.

    Ⓒ Sara has a brother.

    D Sara's other sister is Maria.

    E They have a large garden.

41 ✓

42 Hussein likes books. Usman reads a lot. Usman is Hussein's father.

    A Hussein can read.

    B Hussein just likes looking at the pictures.

    Ⓒ Hussein's dad can read.

    D Usman's cousin is a librarian.

    E Hussein's mother reads a lot.

42 ✓

43 Carly's dad has a butcher's shop. Carly is a plumber. Carly's mum is a secretary.

    A Carly's mum can repair burst pipes.

    B Carly's dad is called Trevor.

    C Carly's dad likes eating steak.

    D Carly's mum keeps secrets.

    Ⓔ Carly's dad sells meat.

43 ✓

44 Molly's mother is in the army. She travels all over the world. She comes home to her family three times a year.

    A Molly's mum is the captain of a ship.

    B Molly travels all over the world.

    C Molly's dad comes home every four months.

    D Molly's mum never sees her daughter.

    Ⓔ Molly sees her mum three times a year.

44 ✓

45 Harry watches a lot of TV. He likes comedy shows best. Mandy is Harry's sister. She hates all TV programmes.

    A Harry's mother is called Mandy.

    B Mandy loves watching the news on TV.

    Ⓒ Harry's favourite TV programmes are funny.

    D Harry's sister has a lot of hobbies.

    E Harry's sister likes documentaries better than comedy shows.

45 ✓

MARK ☐

MARK
✓ OR ✗

Q. 46–50

complete the sentence

Underline **one** word in the brackets to make the sentence sensible.

Example The yacht sailed into the (shop hospital <u>harbour</u> cinema matchbox).

46   The dog lay on the mat and gnawed on a (cat floor emu <u>bone</u> chair).

46   ✓

47   Our car broke down and had to be taken to the (nursery doctor park zoo <u>garage</u>).

47   ✓

48   Potatoes are my favourite (fruit pasta bread pets <u>vegetable</u>).

48   ✓

49   The table was laid, ready for (sanding varnishing <u>lunch</u> painting dancing).

49   ✓

50   Britain is entirely surrounded by (<u>water</u> wasps trees fences lettuce).

50   ✓

Q. 51–55

interpreting tables

Here is a table showing the rainfall in Birmingham and Bristol over a twelve-month period. Look at the table and then answer the questions. Measurements are to the nearest centimetre.

Month	Rainfall in cm	
	Birmingham	Bristol
Jan	17	5
Feb	14	4
Mar	13	4
Apr	9	4
May	9	4
June	8	5
July	10	6
Aug	14	6
Sep	12	5
Oct	13	7
Nov	16	5
Dec	19	6
Total	154	61

51   Which month has the highest rainfall in Bristol?

_____

51

52   Which month has the highest rainfall in Birmingham?

_____

52

53   What is the total of the four months that have the lowest rainfall in Bristol?

_____ cm

53

54   Which month is driest in Birmingham?

_____

54

55   Over the twelve months, which city is drier? _____

55

MARK [ ]

MARK
✓ OR ✗

Q. 56–60

join two words to make one

Circle **one** word from **each** group, which together will make a longer word.

Example (pond (dam) river)   (era down (age))

56 (zip weigh but)   (tonne gram ton)   56

57 (van car round)   (go come tor)   57

58 (super great marvel)   (louse market shop)   58

59 (suit look foot)   (tie over ball)   59

60 (eye make-up brow)   (foot touch sight)   60

Q. 61–65

letters for numbers

If A is **1**, B is **4**, C is **5**, D is **10** and E is **15**, work out these calculations. Give the answer as a letter.

Example C + D = ☐   ___E___

61 $3 \times C = $ ☐   _____   61

62 $E - C = $ ☐   _____   62

63 $A \times C = $ ☐   _____   63

64 $A + B = $ ☐   _____   64

65 $E \div C = B - $ ☐   _____   65

Q. 66–70

antonyms

Underline two words, **one** from **each** set of brackets, that have the **opposite** meaning.

Example (happy kind grin)   (sad face cheerful)

66 (in up down)   (there gone out)   66

67 (bulb sun light)   (dark night day)   67

68 (ugly lean fall)   (fat think meat)   68

69 (out shout move)   (hiss bawl whisper)   69

70 (shut open down)   (wide hear close)   70

MARK ☐

MARK
✓ OR ✗

Q. 71–75

number connections

Start in the shaded square in each grid. Find out how the items in the grid are related to one another. Then fill in the missing item.

71

6	12	18
48	■	
42	36	30

72

42	49	56
35	■	7
	21	14

73

100		80
30	■	70
40	50	60

74

	÷	×
−	■	−
×	÷	+

75

7	8	15
	■	23
99	61	38

71 ☐
72 ☐
73 ☐
74 ☐
75 ☐

Q. 76–80

mixed-up groups

Two groups of three words have been mixed up in each question. Work out which would be the **middle** word in each group if they were in the correct order. Underline these **two** words.

Example city   <u>adolescent</u>   village   <u>town</u>   infant   adult

76	seven	first	third	five	three	second	76 ☐
77	higher	low	high	lowest	lower	highest	77 ☐
78	cat	melon	horse	apple	mouse	blackberry	78 ☐
79	bottom	shout	middle	top	whisper	say	79 ☐
80	fifteenth	five	tenth	fifth	ten	fifteen	80 ☐

Q. 81–85

analogies

Complete these analogies. Write the answers on the lines.

Example Arrive is to depart as come is to _____go_____.

81   March is to May as October is to _____.   81 ☐

82   Six is to sixty as eight is to _____.   82 ☐

83   Fish is to swim as bird is to _____.   83 ☐

84   Eat is to hungry as drink is to _____.   84 ☐

85   Sheep is to mutton as cow is to _____.   85 ☐

MARK ☐

MARK
✓ OR ✗

Q. 86–90
odd ones out

One word in each question does **not** belong with the rest. Underline this word.

Example horrid   nasty   <u>kind</u>   mean   unfriendly

86	daughter	wife	sister	aunt	niece	son	86
87	mastiff	tabby	setter	spaniel	corgi	dachshund	87
88	seven	nineteen	fourth	fifty	eight	twenty	88
89	tiger	leopard	lion	panther	hyena	lynx	89
90	piece	fragment	whole	part	portion	bit	90

Q. 91–95
mixed-up
sentences

Two words must swap places for each sentence to make sense. Underline these **two** words in each sentence.

Example The <u>bone</u> growled softly as he approached the <u>dog</u>.

91	The letters brought the postman to our house.	91
92	Our milkman bit the dog as he opened the front gate.	92
93	Mum asked Olga to help with her homework.	93
94	The warm made the room very fire.	94
95	A cloud of flames arose from the smoke of the bonfire.	95

Q. 96–100
alphabetical
order

Number the words in each line in alphabetical order. Use the alphabet to help you.

Example   HIGH   LOUD   TAKE   FAIL   MEAL
              [2]   [3]   [5]   [1]   [4]

A B C D E F G H I J K L M N O P Q R S T U V W X Y Z

96	WELL	TELL	BELL	SELL	DELL	96
97	GREEN	VIOLET	PURPLE	ORANGE	BLUE	97
98	BREEZE	BRIGHT	BRAVE	BROTHER	BRUSH	98
99	TREE	PROUD	FRIGHT	CRINGE	BRAIN	99
100	START	STAMP	STAIR	STABLE	STALE	100

MARK

END OF TEST

PAPER 1 TOTAL MARK

Q. 1–5

sorting
information

Read the information below carefully. Then answer the questions.

My name is James. I will be 20 in nine years' time. My brother Henry will be 11 then and my sister Eve will be 18. Dad is two years older than Mum who will then be 41.

1	How old am I now?	_____ years old	1 ☐
2	How old is Henry now?	_____ years old	2 ☐
3	How old is Eve now?	_____ years old	3 ☐
4	How old is Mum now?	_____ years old	4 ☐
5	How old is Dad now?	_____ years old	5 ☐

Q. 6–10

letter
sequences

Write the next two items in each sequence. Use the alphabet to help you.

Example AB   CD   EF   GH   __IJ__   __KL__

A B C D E F G H I J K L M N O P Q R S T U V W X Y Z

6	C	F	I	L	_____	_____	6 ☐
7	BC	EF	HI	KL	_____	_____	7 ☐
8	CDE	GHI	KLM	OPQ	_____	_____	8 ☐
9	KL	IJ	GH	EF	_____	_____	9 ☐
10	I	L	O	R	_____	_____	10 ☐

Q. 11–15

which word

One word in each question **cannot** be made from the word in CAPITALS. Underline this word. You may only use each letter once.

Example AIRPORT   rip   <u>park</u>   trio   pair   roar

11	TERRIBLE	tribe	rite	enter	reel	biter	11 ☐
12	CURTAINS	stain	strain	rust	carts	station	12 ☐
13	SERPENT	repent	parent	trees	present	tense	13 ☐
14	TRIANGLE	learn	tinge	gear	tearing	ranger	14 ☐
15	ASSEMBLE	bless	least	beams	measles	seals	15 ☐

MARK [   ]

MARK
✓ OR ✗

Q. 16–20 make a word	Look at how the second word is made from the first word in each pair. Complete the third pair in the same way. Write the answers on the lines.	
	Example (rat rates) (mop mopes) (fin ___fines___)	
	16 (on one) (mat mate) (past _____)	16 ☐
	17 (post poster) (fast faster) (quick _____)	17 ☐
	18 (tot pop) (slit slip) (totter _____)	18 ☐
	19 (bat bare) (scab scare) (dip _____)	19 ☐
	20 (duty dusty) (rut rust) (cot _____)	20 ☐

Q. 21–25 word categories

Below this table are 10 words. Write each word in the correct column.

21 flowers	22 vegetables	23 dogs	24 counties	25 countries

onion   boxer   Durham   Poland   broccoli
daffodil   Italy   gladiolus   terrier   Berkshire

21 ☐
22 ☐
23 ☐
24 ☐
25 ☐

Q. 26–30 jumbled words in sentences

The letters of the words in CAPITALS have been mixed up. Write the **two** correct words on the lines.

Example The TERWA was too cold to WSIM in. ___WATER___ and ___SWIM___

26   The OXF chased the SHEN around the farmyard.

_____ and _____

26 ☐

27   He burned his FRINGES when he picked up the hot STOAT.

_____ and _____

27 ☐

28   The decorator spilled the INAPT all over the PETCAR.

_____ and _____

28 ☐

29   Those NURNESR won a LAMED at the Olympics.

_____ and _____

29 ☐

30   He opened the STAGE so that he could drive his ARC up to the house.

_____ and _____

30 ☐

MARK ☐

MARK
✓ OR ✗

Q. 31–35

match the codes

The words below have been written in code. Which code belongs to which word? Write the answers on the lines.

TIME	EMIT	ITEM	MITE	TAME
4 2 8 6	2 9 6 8	8 6 4 2	2 4 6 8	6 4 2 8

31 The code for TIME is _____ . **31** ☐

32 The code for EMIT is _____ . **32** ☐

33 The code for ITEM is _____ . **33** ☐

34 The code for MITE is _____ . **34** ☐

35 The code for TAME is _____ . **35** ☐

Q. 36–40

word connections

Underline the **one** word that fits with **both** pairs of words in brackets.

Example (heart club) (ruby emerald)   jewel brain <u>diamond</u> card brooch

36 (dahlia snowdrop) (lifted elevated)   upwards crocus rose flower heavy **36** ☐

37 (leash rein) (iron tin)   dog shower clothes beans lead **37** ☐

38 (house bungalow) (even level)   hotel hilly odd flat apartment **38** ☐

39 (below underneath) (miserable sad)   beneath low grumpy cellar tunnel **39** ☐

40 (game challenge) (same equal)   tennis match different plus ground **40** ☐

Q. 41–45

jumbled words in grids

The letters in each grid make **two** four-letter words. The letters must stay in the same columns. Work out where each letter goes.

Example

w	a	l	k
s	w	i	m
s	a	i	k
w	w	l	m

41

m	i	u	r
y	o	n	e

42

t	e	a	l
h	a	i	d

41 ☐

42 ☐

43

p	c	i	e
a	a	h	n

44

f	e	a	h
s	i	s	l

45

w	a	m	t
c	e	n	e

43 ☐

44 ☐

45 ☐

MARK ☐

MARK
✓ OR ✗

Q. 46–50

time problems

Study this train timetable. Then answer the questions below.

Station		Train A	Train B	Train C	Train D
Ashlow	departs	07:13	08:17		11:04
Barston	arrives	07:25		09:33	11:16
Craigow	arrives	07:50	08:54		11:41
Deston	arrives	07:59		10:03	
Earlstown	arrives	08:12	09:16	10:16	12:10

46 Trains A and B both take 59 minutes to travel the same journey. What time does Train B arrive at Barston? _____ 46 ☐

47 What time does Train B arrive at Deston? _____ 47 ☐

48 All four trains take 12 minutes to travel from Ashlow to Barston. What time does Train C leave Ashlow? _____ 48 ☐

49 How many minutes less than Train A does Train C take to complete the whole journey? _____ min 49 ☐

50 Which train takes the longest time to travel from Ashlow to Earlstown? Train _____ 50 ☐

Q. 51–55

analogies

Underline **one** word in **each** set of brackets to complete these analogies.

Example Arrive is to (<u>depart</u> plane speed) as come is to (run hurry <u>go</u>).

51 Top is to (up down bottom) as narrow is to (thin wide short). 51 ☐

52 Grass is to (mow lawn green) as sky is to (cloudy blue sun). 52 ☐

53 Shoal is to (fish shovel whales) as pack is to (luggage puppies dogs). 53 ☐

54 Always is to (sometimes usually never) as often is to (seldom now go). 54 ☐

55 Tadpole is to (kipper swim frog) as caterpillar is to (butterfly grub bird). 55 ☐

Q. 56–60

word meanings

Each of these words can have **two** meanings. Write the numbers of the two meanings in the table below.

Example	56	57	58	59	60
organ	hail	hide	over	cow	blunt
11 12					

Meanings 1 to conceal 2 concluded 3 to subdue 4 to greet
5 saying what you really mean 6 above 7 not sharp
8 animal skin 9 wintry rain 10 a female animal
11 a musical instrument 12 part of the body

56 ☐
57 ☐
58 ☐
59 ☐
60 ☐

MARK ☐

MARK
✓ OR ✗

Q. 61–65

odd ones out

One word in each question does **not** belong with the rest. Underline this word.

Example horrid   nasty   <u>kind</u>   mean   unfriendly

61	table	chair	wardrobe	cooker	bed	sideboard	61
62	robin	starling	ostrich	sparrow	eagle	swift	62
63	bread	butter	cream	milk	yoghurt	cheese	63
64	trawler	warship	pedalo	liner	lifeboat	cruiser	64
65	netball	bowls	darts	tennis	cricket	rugby	65

Q. 66–70

antonyms

Underline the **two** words in each question that have the **opposite** meaning.

Example <u>happy</u>   kind   grin   <u>sad</u>   face   cheerful

66	water low shallow cold deep empty wet swim	66
67	top over throw high tunnel under across cellar	67
68	scribble mucky understand untidy bedroom neat dirty	68
69	assault fight battle attack peace compliment insult shout	69
70	illness trivial great serious angry apologise miner stop	70

Q. 71–75

mixed-up sentences

Two words must swap places for each sentence to make sense. Underline these **two** words in each sentence.

Example The <u>bone</u> growled softly as he approached the <u>dog</u>.

71	The river over the bridge had to be closed.	71
72	The plane used the carpenter to smooth the wood.	72
73	I shouted at her to crossroad at the busy stop.	73
74	Please money as much give as you can.	74
75	Month is the second February of the year.	75

MARK

MARK
✓ OR ✗

Q. 76–80

interpreting graphs

This chart shows the number of children in Years 3 to 6 at a school. Study the chart. Then answer the questions.

The number of children in Years 3 to 6

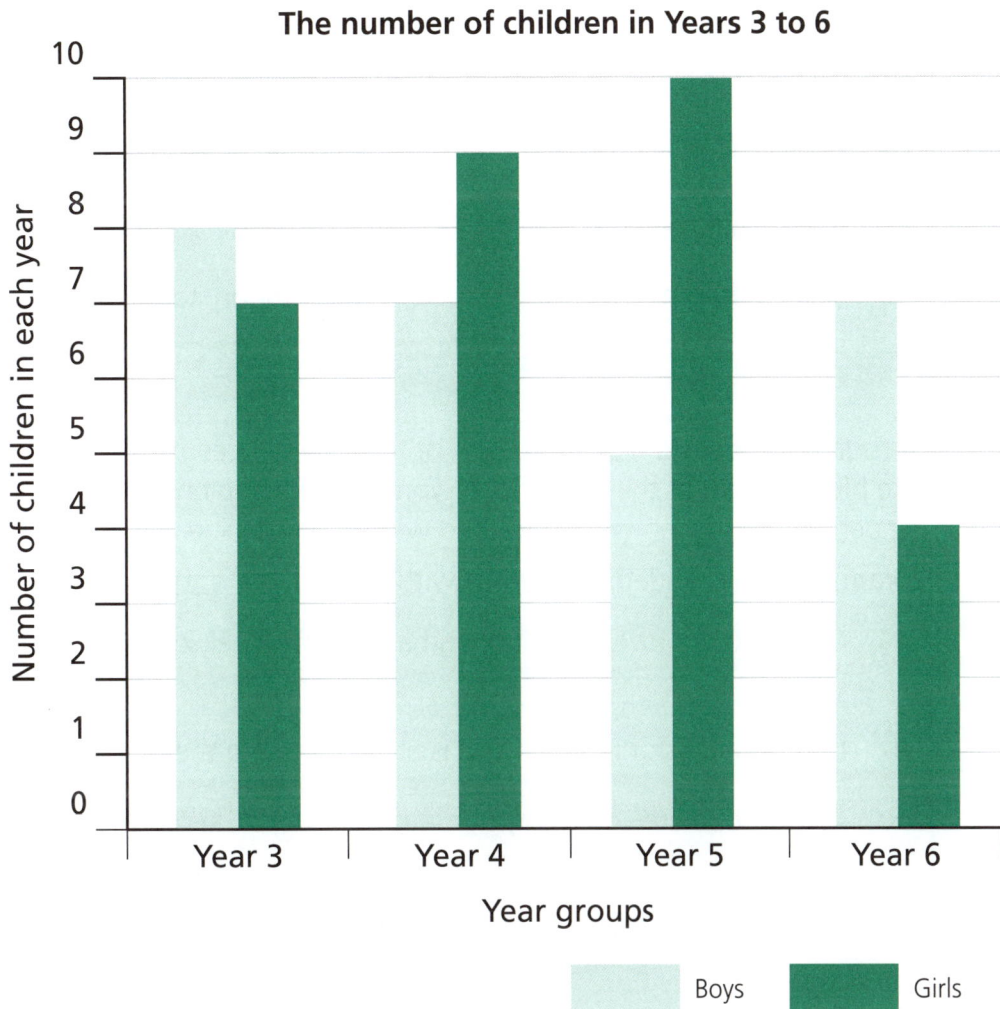

Year groups

Boys   Girls

76 In which two years are there the same number of boys?

Years _____ and _____   76

77 Which year has the most children in it?   Year _____   77

78 How many boys altogether are there in the four years?   _____   78

79 How many girls altogether are there in the four years?   _____   79

80 Which year has the lowest number of children in it?   Year _____   80

MARK

MARK
✓ OR ✗

Q. 81–85

join two words to make one

Circle **one** word from **each** group, which together will make a longer word.

Example (pond (dam) river)   (era   down (age))

81	(fire leg arm)	(foot gun chair)	81 ☐
82	(bar rod row)	(gain knee oar)	82 ☐
83	(by hill half)	(pass near past)	83 ☐
84	(wrong all rail)	(right gone way)	84 ☐
85	(more after before)	(noon tar tea)	85 ☐

Q. 86–90

spot the word

A four-letter word is hidden in each of these sentences. You will find the hidden word at the end of one word and the beginning of the next. Underline the hidden word and then write it on the line.

Example Daniel <u>end</u>ed the speech with a joke.   <u>lend</u>

86   Owing to her lovely singing Emma won the local song competition.

_____   86 ☐

87   Lin's dog doesn't like cats and is always chasing them. _____   87 ☐

88   "What rope are you using to climb that rock?" asked the instructor.

_____   88 ☐

89   "It's raining so pull the hood up over your head," my friend advised.

_____   89 ☐

90   The gang was engaged in crime all round the town.   _____   90 ☐

Q. 91–95

jumbled words with clues

Each question has a word in CAPITALS. The letters in this word have been mixed up. Use the clue to work out what the word is. Write it on the line.

Example NIBOR   (a bird)   <u>ROBIN</u>

91	OSCID (where you can dance)	_____	91 ☐
92	SLIME (a very long way)	_____	92 ☐
93	GERRYUS (where you visit the doctor)	_____	93 ☐
94	EVLITSEINO (what you watch)	_____	94 ☐
95	QUOITEUB (a shop)	_____	95 ☐

MARK ☐

MARK
✓ OR ✗

Q. 96–100

word grids

Fit each set of words into the grid above them. The words should read across and down.

96

ova   lap   pep
ave   pop   pal

97

dog   met   get
are   dam   ore

98

pea   pat   ace
tee   arc   ere

96 ☐

97 ☐

98 ☐

99

tad   ado   ego
ate   gag   aga

100

thy   has   ash
hat   sky   ask

99 ☐

100 ☐

MARK ☐

END OF TEST

PAPER 2 TOTAL MARK ☐

Q. 1–5 spot the word	A four-letter word is hidden in each of these sentences. You will find the hidden word at the end of one word and the beginning of the next. Underline the hidden word and then write it on the line.

Example Daniel <u>end</u>ed the speech with a joke. _____lend_____

1   My friend Oscar trains with his football team every week. _____   1 ☐

2   The caramel truffles were enjoyed by all the class. _____   2 ☐

3   If this reservoir freezes now it could be dangerous. _____   3 ☐

4   The snake goes for the kill in a split second. _____   4 ☐

5   "North is always opposite to south," she said. _____   5 ☐

Q. 6–10 word connections	Underline the **one** word that fits with **both** pairs of words in brackets.

Example (heart club) (ruby emerald)   jewel brain <u>diamond</u> card brooch

6   (shovel digger) (choose select)   make pick grab excavate sell   6 ☐

7   (alter adapt) (coins money)   modify notes pound change destroy   7 ☐

8   (pale faint) (brilliance brightness)   skinny bulb light small candle   8 ☐

9   (piece fragment) (separate disconnect)   split peace whole part bit   9 ☐

10   (college academy) (herd flock)   group set litter crowd school   10 ☐

Q. 11–15 complete the sentence	Underline **one** word in **each** set of brackets to make the sentence sensible.

Example The (plumber <u>electrician</u> baker) repaired the (<u>light</u> loaf sink) so that we could (lamp hear <u>see</u>) again.

11   The (whale goldfish diver) swam round and round its (saucer teacup bowl) and kept the (sharks children weeds) happy.   11 ☐

12   I (were weren't wasn't) too (sad poorly happy) when the late (bus cabbage rocket) made me miss the opening of the show.   12 ☐

13   Rebecca likes (mining gardening reading) and goes to the (hospital library jail) every (century decade week).   13 ☐

14   The (scooter train bicycle) stopped at the (station pool newsagent) to let the (tigers acrobats passengers) get off.   14 ☐

15   Lexi told her (foot mother budgie) that the (taxi restaurant penguin) had (fallen flown arrived).   15 ☐

MARK ☐

MARK
✓ OR ✗

Q. 16–20

word categories

Underline the **general** word in each row, which is the word that includes all the others.

Example banana   apple   <u>fruit</u>   raspberry   pear   kiwi

16   van   car   bus   lorry   ambulance   vehicle | 16 ☐

17   turkey   poultry   chicken   duck   pheasant   goose | 17 ☐

18   hat   cap   bowler   beret   trilby   beanie | 18 ☐

19   hyphen   comma   apostrophe   colon   bracket   punctuation | 19 ☐

20   circle   square   polygon   rectangle   shape   octagon | 20 ☐

Q. 21–25

word meanings

Each of these words can have **two** meanings. Write the numbers of the two meanings in the table below.

Example	**21**	**22**	**23**	**24**	**25**
organ	mean	train	safe	band	drive
11 12					

Meanings   1 secure   2 intend   3 a group of musicians
4 to educate   5 a place to keep money   6 miserly
7 the road up to a house   8 a flat strip of cloth
9 to operate a vehicle   10 transport on rails
11 a musical instrument   12 part of the body

21 ☐
22 ☐
23 ☐
24 ☐
25 ☐

Q. 26–30

word chains

Turn the word on the left into the word on the right. You can only change one letter at a time. Each change must result in a real word.

Example LID   <u>LED</u>   BED

26   D I N   _____   B A N | 26 ☐

27   S I T   _____   H A T | 27 ☐

28   D I G   _____   L O G | 28 ☐

29   M A D   _____   B I D | 29 ☐

30   L O W   _____   R A W | 30 ☐

MARK ☐

MARK
✓ OR ✗

Q. 31–35

change a word

One word is incorrect in each sentence. Underline this word. Write the correct word on the line.

Example Climbing over that wall is not <u>aloud</u>.   <u>allowed</u>

31 The doctor told me to take two of the tables each day.

_____ | 31 |

32 What you have just said is absolute nuisance.   _____ | 32 |

33 The bugler broke into the house when the owners went on holiday.

_____ | 33 |

34 The dog jumped into the pound and swam to the other side.

_____ | 34 |

35 In autumn the loaves fall from the trees.   _____ | 35 |

Q. 36–40

mixed-up groups

Two groups of three words have been mixed up in each question. Work out which would be the **middle** word in each group if they were in the correct order. Underline these **two** words.

Example city   <u>adolescent</u>   village   <u>town</u>   infant   adult

36	wren	monkey	shrew	emu	elephant	eagle		36
37	trickle	chapter	river	stream	page	book		37
38	thinner	sea	lake	thinnest	thin	pool		38
39	second	week	hour	minute	year	day		39
40	midnight	grey	white	dusk	black	dawn		40

Q. 41–45

always has

Look at the word in **bold**. Underline **one** option in the brackets. It must describe what the word in bold **always has**.

Example A **lake** always has (boats   <u>water</u>   ducks   swimmers   fish).

41 **Money** always has (paper   metal   a bank   value   an account   a wallet). | 41 |

42 A **box** always has (a lid   hinges   a Jack   volume   wheels   wood). | 42 |

43 A **bookcase** always has (books   ornaments   clutter   shelves   legs). | 43 |

44 **Water** is always (hot   cold   clean   dirty   wet   deep   green). | 44 |

45 A **pair** always has (fruit   socks   double   two   three   trousers). | 45 |

MARK [   ]

MARK
✓ OR ✗

Q. 46–50

move a letter

Take **one** letter from the first word and put it in the second word to make two new words. Write the letter you have moved and the two new words in the table below.

	First word	Second word	Letter moved	New first word	New second word
Example	slope	feat	s	lope	feast
46	cause	bond			
47	store	rifle			
48	pretty	gain			
49	coast	sets			
50	zone	pries			

46 ☐
47 ☐
48 ☐
49 ☐
50 ☐

Q. 51–55

missing three-letter words

Use the clue to work out the five-letter word. The missing three letters also form a word. Write the three-letter word on the line.

Example S _ _ _ T   (to begin)   TAR

51   S _ _ _ L   (to take something from someone else)   _____   51 ☐

52   S _ _ _ E   (a large pebble)   _____   52 ☐

53   C _ _ _ Y   (a sweet)   _____   53 ☐

54   B _ _ _ E   (a woman getting married)   _____   54 ☐

55   G _ _ _ M   (to shine)   _____   55 ☐

Q. 56–60

letters for numbers

If A is **1**, B is **2**, C is **3**, D is **5** and E is **10**, work out these calculations. Give the answer as a letter.

Example C + B = _D_

56   B × C = D + ☐   _____   56 ☐

57   D – C = ☐   _____   57 ☐

58   E ÷ D = ☐   _____   58 ☐

59   A + B + C = D + ☐   _____   59 ☐

60   A × B × C × D = 3 × ☐   _____   60 ☐

MARK ☐

MARK
✓ OR ✗

Q. 61–65

add a letter

Read the clue in brackets. Add **one** letter to the word in CAPITALS to make a new word that matches the clue. Write the new word on the line.

Example CANE   (lifts heavy objects)   <u>CRANE</u>

61   PLAN   (flatland)   _____   61

62   TANK   (be grateful)   _____   62

63   SALE   (not fresh)   _____   63

64   AMPLE   (an example or specimen)   _____   64

65   IDEA   (perfect)   _____   65

Q. 66–70

position problems

This is a diagram of a five-storey block of flats. Families A, B, C, D and E live here. Work out where each family lives. Write the letter of the family on the correct floor in the diagram.

Family B lives three floors above Family E.

Family E has no stairs to climb in order to get home.

Family D lives two floors below Family C.

Family C has to climb the most stairs.

Family A has to climb one flight of stairs to get home.

	Floor	Family
66	4th floor	
67	3rd floor	
68	2nd floor	
69	1st floor	
70	Ground floor	

66

67

68

69

70

MARK [ ]

MARK
✓ OR ✗

Q. 71–75

word codes

Work out these codes. The code used in each question is different. Use the alphabet to help you.

A B C D E F G H I J K L M N O P Q R S T U V W X Y Z

Example If DWU is the code for BUS, what does EQCEJ mean? ___COACH___

71   If IBQQZ is the code for HAPPY, what does KPZGVM mean?

_____   71 ☐

72   If VKTGF is the code for TIRED, what does YGCTA mean?

_____   72 ☐

73   If RSZKD is the code for STALE, what does EQDRG mean?

_____   73 ☐

74   If ITGGP is the code for GREEN, what does AGNNQY mean?

_____   74 ☐

75   If CHEUD is the code for ZEBRA, what does WLJHU mean?

_____   75 ☐

Q. 76–80

join two words to make one

Circle **one** word from **each** group, which together will make a longer word.

Example (pond (dam) river)   (era down (age))

76 (over under below)	(stand sit crouch)	76 ☐
77 (more plus extra)	(usual normal ordinary)	77 ☐
78 (cot divan bed)	(age time blanket)	78 ☐
79 (shower sink bath)	(cubicle swim room)	79 ☐
80 (eat sup drink)	(pose glass dinner)	80 ☐

MARK ☐

MARK
✓ OR ✗

Q. 81–85

odd ones out

One word in each question does **not** belong with the rest. Underline this word.

Example horrid   nasty   <u>kind</u>   mean   unfriendly

81	Sheffield	England	London	Leeds	Coventry	Exeter	81 ☐
82	lollipop	coffee	sherbet	toffee	humbug	gobstopper	82 ☐
83	violin	cello	guitar	trumpet	harp	viola	83 ☐
84	tortoise	lizard	viper	chameleon	rabbit	crocodile	84 ☐
85	Himalayas	Andes	Pennines	Rockies	Alps	Thames	85 ☐

Q. 86–90

jumbled words in sentences

The letters of the words in CAPITALS have been mixed up. Write the **two** correct words on the lines.

Example The TERWA was too cold to WSIM in. ___<u>WATER</u>___ and ___<u>SWIM</u>___

86   Binoy scored three GAOLS in the CATHM.

_____ and _____   86 ☐

87   I read the GAPES as fast as I could to FISHIN the book.

_____ and _____   87 ☐

88   He pricked his finger on the SORE and hoped it would not leave a CARS.

_____ and _____   88 ☐

89   The CHEATER told the children to be QUITE.

_____ and _____   89 ☐

90   Annie likes to KIPS and play out in the DANGER.

_____ and _____   90 ☐

MARK ☐

Verbal Reasoning
Progress Papers 1
Answers

Schofield & Sims

Verbal Reasoning Progress Papers 1

Notes for parents, tutors, teachers and other helpers

This pull-out book contains correct answers to all the questions in **Verbal Reasoning Progress Papers 1**, and is designed to assist you, the adult helper, as you mark the child's work. Once the child has become accustomed to the method of working, you may wish to give him or her direct access to this pull-out section.

When marking, put a tick or a cross in the tinted column on the far right of the question page. **Only one mark is available for each question**. Sub-total boxes at the foot of each page will help you to add marks quickly. You can then fill in the total marks at the end of the paper. The total score is out of 100 and can easily be turned into a percentage. The child's progress can be recorded using the **Progress chart** on page 52.

The child should aim to spend between 45 and 75 minutes on each paper, but may need more time, or more than one session, to complete the paper. The child should try to work on each paper when feeling fresh and free from distraction.

How to use the pull-out answers

This booklet contains answers to all the questions in the book, as well as footnotes to help with marking. Where the child has answered a question incorrectly, take time to look at the question and answer together and work out how the correct answer was achieved.

By working through the tests and corresponding answers, the child will start to recognise the clues that he or she should look for next time. These skills can then be put into practice by moving on to the next paper, as the difficulty increases incrementally throughout the series.

When a paper has been marked, notice if there are any topics that are proving particularly tricky. You may wish to complete some targeted practice in those areas, by focusing on that particular topic as it appears in each paper. For example, if a child has struggled with word meanings, but answered all other questions accurately, you may wish to target only word meanings questions in your next practice session. The **Topics chart**, available to download for free from the Schofield & Sims website, makes it easy to tailor practice to the child's individual needs.

Paper 1

1 DAM*
2 BREAKFAST*
3 TROUSERS*
4 FLIES*
5 GIRAFFE*

6 colour   paint
7 dog   cat
8 triangle   circle
9 bicycle   sledge
10 table   desk

11 (across) ado can eye
   (down) ace day one
12 (across) bat ago yet
   (down) bay age tot
13 (across) pal ire net
   (down) pin are let
14 (across) not are pen
   (down) nap ore ten
15 (across) par ewe wed
   (down) pew awe red

16 read
17 hero
18 leaf
19 goal
20 soft

21 10
22 9
23 7
24 6
25 1

26 D
27 E
28 W
29 HI
30 U

31 SEED
32 DARE
33 READ
34 HARD
35 EARS

Paper 1 – continued

36 PEA
37 RAT
38 TIN
39 ROW
40 EAR

41 C
42 C
43 E
44 E
45 C

46 bone
47 garage
48 vegetable
49 lunch
50 water

51 October
52 December
53 16cm
54 June
55 Bristol

56 but   ton
57 car   go
58 super   market
59 foot   ball
60 eye   sight

61 E
62 D
63 C
64 C
65 A

66 in   out
67 light   dark
68 lean   fat
69 shout   whisper
70 open   close

71 24 (+6)
72 28 (+7)
73 90 (–10)
74 + (repeating pattern)
75 160 (add the previous number)

Paper 1 – *continued*

76	five	second
77	higher	lower
78	cat	apple
79	middle	say
80	tenth	ten
81	December	
82	eighty	
83	fly	
84	thirsty	
85	beef	
86	son	
87	tabby	
88	fourth	
89	hyena	
90	whole	
91	letters	postman
92	milkman	dog
93	Mum	Olga
94	warm	fire
95	flames	smoke
96	5 4 1 3 2	
97	2 5 4 3 1	
98	2 3 1 4 5	
99	5 4 3 2 1	
100	5 4 2 1 3	

*spellings must be correct

Paper 2

1	11 years old	
2	2 years old	
3	9 years old	
4	32 years old	
5	34 years old	
6	O	R
7	NO	QR
8	STU	WXY
9	CD	AB
10	U	X
11	enter	
12	station	
13	parent	
14	ranger	
15	least	
16	paste	
17	quicker	
18	popper	
19	dire	
20	cost	
21	daffodil	gladiolus
22	onion	broccoli
23	boxer	terrier
24	Durham	Berkshire
25	Poland	Italy
26	FOX	HENS*
27	FINGERS	TOAST*
28	PAINT	CARPET*
29	RUNNERS	MEDAL*
30	GATES	CAR*
31	2468	
32	8642	
33	4286	
34	6428	
35	2968	
36	rose	
37	lead	
38	flat	
39	low	
40	match	

	Paper 2 – *continued*	
41	mine	your*
42	head	tail*
43	pain	ache*
44	fish	seal*
45	went	came*
46	08:29	
47	09:03	
48	09:21	
49	4 min	
50	Train D	
51	bottom	wide
52	green	blue
53	fish	dogs
54	never	seldom
55	frog	butterfly
56	4	9
57	1	8
58	2	6
59	3	10
60	5	7
61	cooker	
62	ostrich	
63	bread	
64	pedalo	
65	darts	
66	shallow	deep
67	over	under
68	untidy	neat
69	compliment	insult
70	trivial	serious
71	river	bridge
72	plane	carpenter
73	crossroad	stop
74	money	give
75	month	February
76	Years 4 and 6	
77	Year 4	
78	27	
79	30	
80	Year 6	

	Paper 2 – *continued*	
81	arm	chair
82	bar	gain
83	by	pass
84	rail	way
85	after	noon
86	also	
87	sand	
88	pear	
89	very	
90	meal	
91	DISCO*	
92	MILES*	
93	SURGERY*	
94	TELEVISION*	
95	BOUTIQUE*	
96	*(across)* pal ova pep *(down)* pop ave lap[†]	
97	*(across)* dog are met *(down)* dam ore get[†]	
98	*(across)* pea arc tee *(down)* pat ere ace[†]	
99	*(across)* aga tad ego *(down)* ate gag ado[†]	
100	*(across)* hat ash sky *(down)* has ask thy[†]	

*spellings must be correct

[†]*across* and *down* words can also be the other way round

Paper 3

1. cart
2. melt
3. snow
4. fort
5. this

6. pick
7. change
8. light
9. part
10. school

11. goldfish bowl children
12. wasn't happy bus
13. reading library week
14. train station passengers
15. mother taxi arrived

16. vehicle
17. poultry
18. hat
19. punctuation
20. shape

21. 2 6
22. 4 10
23. 1 5
24. 3 8
25. 7 9

26. BIN
27. SAT or HIT
28. DOG
29. BAD
30. ROW or LAW

Accept any accurate response to word chain questions.

31. (tables) tablets*
32. (nuisance) nonsense*
33. (bugler) burglar*
34. (pound) pond*
35. (loaves) leaves*

36. monkey eagle
37. chapter stream
38. thinner lake
39. week minute
40. midnight grey

Paper 3 – continued

41. value
42. volume
43. shelves
44. wet
45. two

46. u case bound
47. t sore trifle
    or s tore rifles
48. r petty grain
49. a cost seats
50. z one prizes

51. TEA
52. TON
53. AND
54. RID
55. LEA

56. A
57. B
58. B
59. A
60. E

61. PLAIN
62. THANK
63. STALE
64. SAMPLE
65. IDEAL

66. C
67. B
68. D
69. A
70. E

71. JOYFUL
72. WEARY
73. FRESH
74. YELLOW
75. TIGER

76. under stand
77. extra ordinary
78. bed time
79. bath room
80. sup pose

Paper 3 – *continued*

81	England
82	coffee
83	trumpet
84	rabbit
85	Thames

86	GOALS	MATCH*
87	PAGES	FINISH*
88	ROSE	SCAR*
89	TEACHER	QUIET*
90	SKIP	GARDEN*

91	D
92	E
93	C
94	B
95	B

96	J
97	S
98	no
99	fed
100	E

*spellings must be correct

Paper 4

1	Sat
2	Mon
3	Tues and Thurs
4	£199
5	85

6	wolf	hens*
7	coat	shoe*
8	lose	gain*
9	fast	slow*
10	huge	tiny*

11	VWXYZ
12	VWYZX
13	ZXYWU
14	VYZXU
15	WYVXU

16	butter
17	scar
18	pets
19	sitting
20	meat

21	gain	loss
22	feminine	masculine
23	fine	coarse
24	divide	multiply
25	departure	arrival

26	AT
27	OT
28	BE
29	TE
30	EN

31	FILE	MILE
32	POST	PORT
	or POST	PAST
	or CAST	PAST
33	FARE	PARE
34	COLD	CORD
35	TALE	SALE
	or MILE	MOLE
	or PILE	POLE

Accept any accurate response to word chain questions.

Paper 4 – *continued*

36	7.5 or 7$\frac{1}{2}$	3.75 or 3$\frac{3}{4}$
37	33	41
38	60	48
39	6.25	3.125
40	62	126
41	feel	
42	hate	
43	dash	
44	deny *or* test	
45	your	
46	weep	
47	huge	
48	teaching	
49	held	
50	evil	
51	spend	
52	robot	
53	yarns	
54	stray	
55	dates	
56	water	
57	engine	
58	bakers	
59	my	
60	terrier	
61	depth	
62	wings	
63	a top	
64	pages	
65	an orbit	
66	unknown	
67	unknown	
68	false	
69	true	
70	false	
71	puncture	tyre
72	angel	angle
73	him	I
74	describe	prescribe
75	submarine	trawler

Paper 4 – *continued*

76	LEAP	
77	PLEAD	
78	PEALED	
79	DEAL	
80	PADDLE	
81	occupied	inhabited
82	select	choose
83	dish	bowl
84	frost	ice
85	melody	tune
86	V	Y
87	H16	K19
88	T	J
89	V	X
90	15K	16O
91	TABLE	
92	PEACE	
93	SPLICE	
94	REPLY	
95	CREATE	
96	animal	
97	colour	
98	profession	
99	container	
100	insect	

*spellings must be correct

Paper 5

1	water	blood*
2	sunny	cloud*
3	sweet	round*
4	rough	stone*
5	paint	brush*

6	IT
7	GH
8	NE
9	AD
10	CE

11	hand
12	night
13	pluck
14	see
15	quadruple

16	drag	pull
17	begin	commence
18	relative	relation
19	below	under
20	attempt	try

21	r	fail	horse
22	i	bran	paint
23	u	case	gauze
24	l	idea	flair
25	h	same	thank

26	SCORE*
27	BUILDER*
28	DIFFICULT*
29	COLLECT*
30	PHRASE*

31	break	fast
32	tar	get
33	day	light
34	lamp	shade
35	pot	hole

36	skin
37	tilt
38	over
39	tile
40	read

Paper 5 – *continued*

41	flower
42	tool
43	weapon
44	fabric
45	timber

46	C
47	A
48	C
49	B
50	B

51	6	9
52	5	10
53	3	7
54	1	8
55	2	4

56	37	49
57	32	42
58	43	57
59	31	34
60	17	3

61	D
62	B
63	C
64	D
65	A

66	solution	answer
67	unknown	obscure
68	silence	calm
69	slender	slim
70	restricted	limited

71	sheriff	outlaw	gaol
72	cereal	breakfast	school
73	aunt	mother's	sister
74	pool	water	swimming
75	leap	year	four

76	nation
77	reseed
78	misted
79	noted
80	circled

Paper 5 – continued

81	5 4 2 3 1
82	4 3 5 1 2
83	3 5 2 4 1
84	3 4 1 5 2
85	2 1 3 5 4

86	ART
87	BIT
88	AND
89	ALL
90	RID

91	field	present
92	medium	hill
93	test	queen
94	slice	greener
95	duet	hungry

96	TRAIN	STOPPING*
97	DOCTOR	UNWELL*
98	WAYS	ROAD*
99	FIRST	TEST*
100	FORWARD	HOLIDAY*

*spellings must be correct

Paper 6

1	52
2	67
3	29
4	72
5	17.5 or $17\frac{1}{2}$

6	serious
7	ancient
8	untrustworthy
9	beautiful
10	hidden

11	MALE	MOLE
	or DARE	MARE
12	BARE	CARE
13	PART	DART
	or DARK	DART
14	BARE	FARE
15	RIDE	RITE

Accept any accurate response to word chain questions.

16	melt	freeze
17	friend	foe
18	awake	asleep
19	lenient	strict
20	proud	humble

21	Lucy
22	Amy
23	first floor
24	Kim
25	Sophie

26	MANES
27	NAMES
28	NEAT
29	MEANS
30	STEAM

31	US	TR
32	TU	WX
33	SD	UB
34	ABD	FGI
35	YL	CJ

Paper 6 – *continued*

36	shun *or* mesh *or* ours	
37	scar	
38	land	
39	full	
40	chat	
41	2012	
42	2013	
43	2010	
44	2013	
45	2014	
46	brave	oven
47	shine	into
48	steps	spar
49	trail	pill
50	cakes	meal
51	so	raining
52	mend	broken
53	me	Mum
54	down	up
55	looked	stood
56	kid	calf
57	sprout	leek
58	peach	pear
59	canary	eagle
60	reins	bridle
61	(died) dyed*	
62	(parasol) parachute*	
63	(chum) charm*	
64	(manger) manager*	
65	(suet) suit *or* suite*	
66	sling	
67	fine	
68	port	
69	last	
70	mustard	
71	35	43
72	19	30
73	57	71
74	12	10
75	34	68

Paper 6 – *continued*

76	five		
77	burrow		
78	computer		
79	wire		
80	hand		
81	owlet*		
82	prince*		
83	Earth*		
84	cheese *or* butter*		
85	canal*		
86	servant		
87	mention		
88	singed		
89	idled		
90	terminal		
91	SCENT		
92	TOOTH		
93	BOUGHT		
94	COURT		
95	PALACE		
96	e	star	tear
97	m	cries	seams
98	b	tale	bright
99	f	rat	flint
100	r	tough	grave

*spellings must be correct

This book of answers is a pull-out section from
Verbal Reasoning Progress Papers 1

Published by **Schofield & Sims Ltd,**
7 Mariner Court, Wakefield, West Yorkshire WF4 3FL, UK
Telephone 01484 607080
www.schofieldandsims.co.uk

First published in 2016
This edition copyright © Schofield & Sims Ltd, 2018
Second impression 2018

Author: **Patrick Berry**
Patrick Berry has asserted his moral rights under the Copyright, Designs and
Patents Act, 1988, to be identified as the author of this work.

British Library Cataloguing in Publication Data
A catalogue record for this book is available from the British Library.

Design by **Oxford Designers and Illustrators Ltd**
Printed in the UK by **Page Bros (Norwich) Ltd**

ISBN 978 07217 1470 7

MARK
✓ OR ✗

Q. 91–95

time problems

Here is part of a railway timetable. It shows morning trains from Airevale to Condale, stopping at Burdale on the way.

Circle your answer to each question.

Train	Airevale	Burdale		Condale
	depart	arrive	depart	arrive
A	08:10	08:30	08:35	09:05
B	09:15	09:30	09:35	10:05
C	10:05	10:30	10:35	11:00
D	11:00	11:20	11:35	12:05
E	12:05	12:25	12:30	13:05

91 Which train stops longest at Burdale?   A B C D E   91 ☐

92 Mohammed's journey took one hour, on which train?   A B C D E   92 ☐

93 Which is the fastest train from Burdale to Condale?   A B C D E   93 ☐

94 Which train takes exactly twice as long to travel the second part of the journey as the first?   A B C D E   94 ☐

95 Which is the fastest train from Airevale to Burdale?   A B C D E   95 ☐

Q. 96–100

alphabetical order

Answer the questions. Use the alphabet to help you.

A B C D E F G H I J K L M N O P Q R S T U V W X Y Z

96 Which letter comes after the third vowel?   _____   96 ☐

97 If all the vowels were removed, what would be the 15th letter?   _____   97 ☐

98 Apart from 'hi', what other word of two consecutive letters is found in the alphabet?   _____   98 ☐

99 If you read the alphabet backwards, what word of three consecutive letters can you find?   _____   99 ☐

100 Reading the alphabet backwards, what is the fourth vowel?   _____   100 ☐

MARK ☐

END OF TEST

PAPER 3 TOTAL MARK ☐

Q. 1–5

interpreting graphs

This graph shows the number of DVDs sold in a shop in one week last year. Study the graph. Then answer the questions.

The number of DVDs sold by a shop in one week

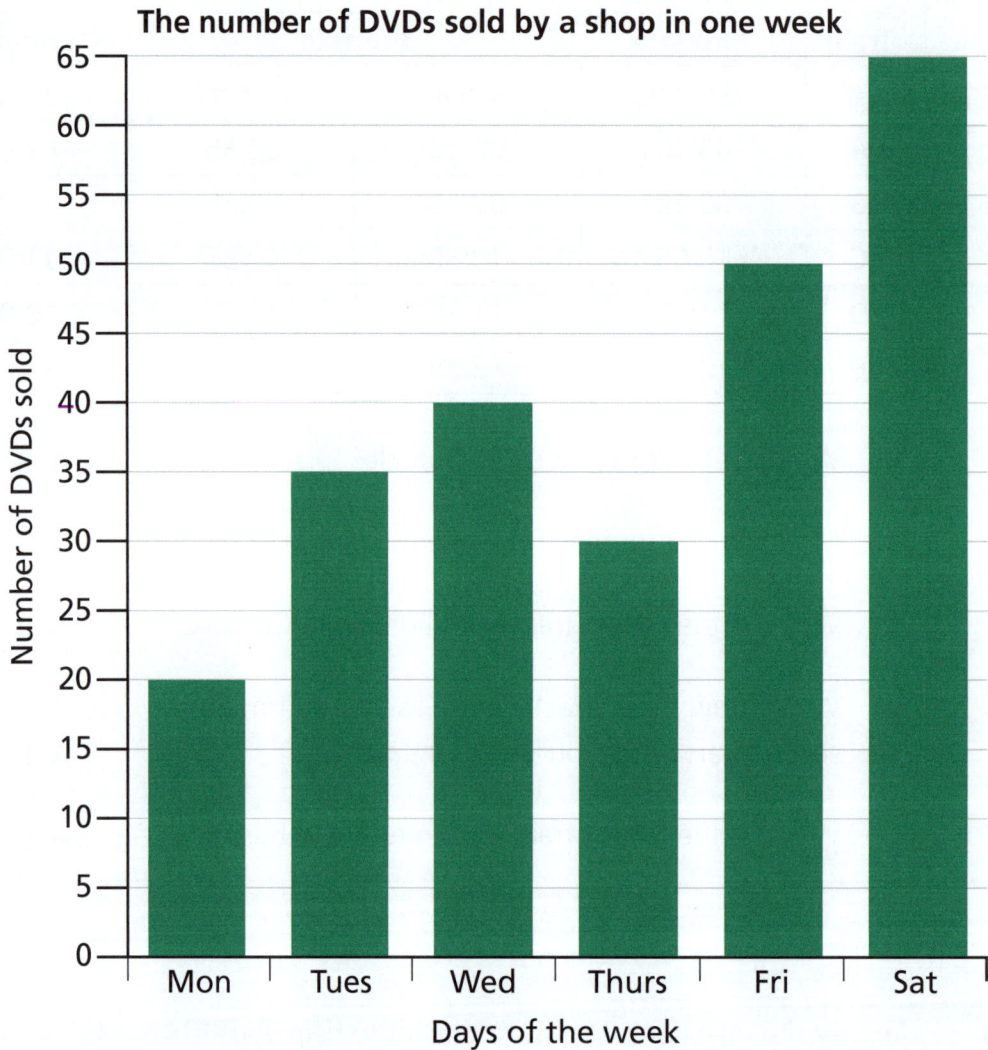

Number of DVDs sold

Days of the week

1 What day of the week was busiest? _____ 1 ☐

2 What was the least busy day? _____ 2 ☐

3 Which two days' sales together equalled Saturday's sales?

_____ and _____ 3 ☐

4 If each DVD cost £9.95, how much money was taken on the Monday of that week? £ _____ 4 ☐

5 How many DVDs were sold altogether on the Monday and Saturday?

_____ 5 ☐

MARK ☐

MARK
✓ OR ✗

Q. 6–10

jumbled words in grids

The letters in each grid make **two** four-letter words. The letters must stay in the same columns. Work out where each letter goes.

Example

w	a	l	k
s	w	i	m
s	a	i	k
w	w	l	m

6

w	e	n	f
h	o	l	s

7

c	h	a	e
s	o	o	t

8

l	o	i	e
g	a	s	n

9

f	l	s	w
s	a	o	t

10

h	i	n	e
t	u	g	y

6 ☐
7 ☐
8 ☐
9 ☐
10 ☐

Q. 11–15

match the codes

The words below have been written in code. Which code belongs to which word? Write the answers on the lines.

GREAT   GRATE   TEARS   GATES   RAGES

VWYZX   WYVXU   VYZXU   VWXYZ   ZXYWU

11 The code for GREAT is _____.

12 The code for GRATE is _____.

13 The code for TEARS is _____.

14 The code for GATES is _____.

15 The code for RAGES is _____.

11 ☐
12 ☐
13 ☐
14 ☐
15 ☐

Q. 16–20

make a word

Look at how the second word is made from the first word in each pair. Complete the third pair in the same way. Write the answers on the lines.

Example (rat rates) (mop mopes) (fin __*fines*__)

16 (old bold)   (ark bark)   (utter _____)

17 (tile stile)   (mile smile)   (car _____)

18 (pans snap)   (mood doom)   (step _____)

19 (upper utter)   (pray tray)   (sipping _____)

20 (bate beat)   (hate heat)   (mate _____)

16 ☐
17 ☐
18 ☐
19 ☐
20 ☐

MARK ☐

MARK
✓ OR ✗

Q. 21–25

antonyms

Underline the **two** words in each question that have the **opposite** meaning.

Example <u>happy</u> kind grin <u>sad</u> face cheerful

21	gamble	gain	dollar	loss	save	bank	invest	21 ☐
22	manly	lady	feminine	female	person	masculine	opposite	22 ☐
23	gently	severe	fine	course	coarse	jagged	plane	23 ☐
24	add	spread	attack	divide	maths	conquer	multiply	24 ☐
25	go	wait	departure	journey	train	station	arrival	25 ☐

Q. 26–30

missing letters

The same **two** letters end the first word and begin the next word. Write the letters.

Example T R A <u>I</u> <u>L</u>   <u>I</u> <u>L</u> L N E S S

26	G R E __ __	__ __ T I C	26 ☐
27	F O __ __	__ __ H E R	27 ☐
28	T R I __ __	__ __ F O R E	28 ☐
29	B I __ __	__ __ E T H	29 ☐
30	L I V __ __	__ __ C L O S E	30 ☐

Q. 31–35

word chains

Turn the word at the top of each grid into the word at the bottom. You can only change one letter at a time. Each change must result in a real word.

Example

T	A	L	E
T	A	K	E
L	A	K	E
L	I	K	E

31

F	I	V	E
M	I	L	D

32

C	O	S	T
P	A	R	T

31 ☐
32 ☐

33

F	A	R	M
P	A	L	E

34

B	O	L	D
C	O	R	E

35

T	I	L	E
S	O	L	E

33 ☐
34 ☐
35 ☐

MARK ☐

MARK
✓ OR ✗

Q. 36–40

number sequences

Write the next two numbers in each sequence.

Example 2 4 6 8 _10_ _12_

36	60	30	15	_____	_____		36
37	9	17	25	_____	_____		37
38	96	84	72	_____	_____		38
39	50.0	25.0	12.5	_____	_____		39
40	2	6	14	30	_____	_____	40

Q. 41–45

spot the word

A four-letter word is hidden in each of these sentences. You will find the hidden word at the end of one word and the beginning of the next. Underline the hidden word and then write it on the line.

Example Daniel ended the speech with a joke. _lend_

41 Joel's concerned wife elbowed her way through the crowd of tourists.

_____ 41

42 "That explanation is not clear enough," repeated the head teacher.

_____ 42

43 You should put only cold ashes in your dustbin. _____ 43

44 The company made nylon kites to send to lots of countries.

_____ 44

45 We could not deny our enjoyment of the practical joke.

_____ 45

Q. 46–50

analogies

Underline **one** word in the brackets to complete these analogies.

Example Arrive is to depart as come is to (run hurry go hide).

46 Happy is to smile as unhappy is to (yell shout miserable weep anger). 46

47 Wide is to narrow as tiny is to (small huge minute scarce little). 47

48 Chef is to cookery as professor is to (sewing frying chemistry teaching). 48

49 Is is to was as hold is to (grab throw held bowled carry). 49

50 Part is to trap as live is to (vile dead snare evil victim). 50

MARK ☐

MARK
✓ OR ✗

Q. 51–55

crosswords

Look at the clues. Write in the answers.

		e		
	■	m	■	
		b		
	■	e	■	
		r		

(Grid with numbers: 1 top-left, 2 top-right, 3 left third row, 4 left bottom row)

51	**1 across** to pay out money	51 ☐
52	**3 across** a mechanical human	52 ☐
53	**4 across** sewing or knitting threads	53 ☐
54	**1 down** to wander away	54 ☐
55	**2 down** times of historical events	55 ☐

Q. 56–60

complete the sentence

Underline **one** word in the brackets to make the sentence sensible.

Example The yacht sailed into the (shop hospital <u>harbour</u> cinema matchbox).

56	Firefighters use (water drills engines) to put out fires.	56 ☐
57	The mechanic could not start the car's (driver engine windscreen tyre).	57 ☐
58	Flour is used by (florists bakers penguins) to make bread.	58 ☐
59	I am (my their her) parents' only child.	59 ☐
60	The driver was bitten by the (tenor terrier terror terrain tepid).	60 ☐

Q. 61–65

always has

Look at the word in **bold**. Underline **one** option in the brackets. It must describe what the word in bold **always has**.

Example A **lake** always has (boats <u>water</u> ducks swimmers fish).

61	A **pond** always has (frogs birds rushes pebbles waves depth).	61 ☐
62	A **bird** always has (eggs a nest a tree wings flight seed).	62 ☐
63	A **table** always has (food a tablecloth cutlery chairs a top diners).	63 ☐
64	A **book** always has (a title pages a story writing an author a reader).	64 ☐
65	A **planet** always has (water air people an orbit heat).	65 ☐

MARK ☐

MARK
✓ OR ✗

Q. 66–70

sorting information

Read the information below carefully. Tick (✓) true, false or unknown for each statement. Tick **one** only.

My name is Lucas. My brother is Jack. My sister is Grace. Our parents have never separated. My friend is Freddie. Our mother is Jo and our father is Michael. My aunt and uncle are Gill and Peter. Katy is our next door neighbour.

		true	false	unknown	
66	Freddie is Katy's son.	☐	☐	☐	66 ☐
67	Gill is my mother's sister.	☐	☐	☐	67 ☐
68	Freddie is my father.	☐	☐	☐	68 ☐
69	Jack is Michael's son.	☐	☐	☐	69 ☐
70	Lucas is my father.	☐	☐	☐	70 ☐

Q. 71–75

mixed-up sentences

Two words must swap places for each sentence to make sense. Underline these **two** words in each sentence.

Example The <u>bone</u> growled softly as he approached the <u>dog</u>.

71 We could not use the car because the puncture had a tyre. 71 ☐

72 In the angel where the two walls met stood the statue of an angle. 72 ☐

73 Him asked I for a packet of chocolate biscuits. 73 ☐

74 The doctor said she could not describe any medication unless I could prescribe my symptoms. 74 ☐

75 Unlike a submarine, a trawler can travel under water. 75 ☐

Q. 76–80

symbol codes

The word **PEDAL** is written as ◀ ■ ▲ ▶ ♦ in code. Use the same code to work out the hidden words.

76 ♦ ■ ▶ ◀ _____ 76 ☐

77 ◀ ♦ ■ ▶ ▲ _____ 77 ☐

78 ◀ ■ ▶ ♦ ■ ▲ _____ 78 ☐

79 ▲ ■ ▶ ♦ _____ 79 ☐

80 ◀ ▶ ▲ ▲ ♦ ■ _____ 80 ☐

MARK ☐

MARK
✓ OR ✗

Q. 81–85

synonyms

Underline two words, **one** from **each** set of brackets, that are **similar** in meaning.

Example (large great <u>tiny</u> huge)   (box <u>small</u> hungry crate)

81 (occupied home empty address)   (away garden inhabited full)   81 ☐

82 (shop buy discard select)   (sell deal choose bargain)   82 ☐

83 (dish plate cup mug)   (knife fork bowl crockery)   83 ☐

84 (season frost weather heat)   (cold ice month spring)   84 ☐

85 (music melody pianist composer)   (song symphony sing tune)   85 ☐

Q. 86–90

letter sequences

Write the next two items in each sequence. Use the alphabet to help you.

Example AB   CD   EF   GH   <u>IJ</u>   <u>KL</u>

A B C D E F G H I J K L M N O P Q R S T U V W X Y Z

86 G   J   M   P   S   _____   _____   86 ☐

87 S1   V4   Y7   B10   E13   _____   _____   87 ☐

88 A   Z   D   W   G   _____   _____   88 ☐

89 G   I   L   N   Q   S   _____   _____   89 ☐

90 7Q   9U   10Y   12C   13G   _____   _____   90 ☐

Q. 91–95

add a letter

Read the clue in brackets. Add **one** letter to the word in CAPITALS to make a new word that matches the clue. Write the new word on the line.

Example CANE   (lifts heavy objects)   <u>CRANE</u>

91 TALE   (an article of furniture)   _____   91 ☐

92 PACE   (the opposite of war)   _____   92 ☐

93 SPICE   (to unite or join together)   _____   93 ☐

94 RELY   (an answer or acknowledgement)   _____   94 ☐

95 CRATE   (to invent, make or produce)   _____   95 ☐

MARK ☐

MARK
✓ OR ✗

Q. 96–100 word categories	Underline the **general** word in each row, which is the word that includes all the others.					
	Example banana apple fruit raspberry pear kiwi					
96	goat	dog	rabbit	animal	cow	sheep	96
97	red	colour	yellow	brown	vermillion	pink	97
98	music	law	teaching	profession	architecture	medicine	98
99	jug	bucket	bowl	can	bottle	container	99
100	fly	insect	ant	wasp	mosquito	beetle	100

MARK

END OF TEST   PAPER 4 TOTAL MARK

START HERE

Q. 1–5

jumbled words in grids

The letters in each grid make **two** five-letter words. The letters must stay in the same columns. Work out where each letter goes.

Example

c	l	o	w	n
f	r	u	i	t
c	r	o	w	t
f	l	u	i	n

1

b	l	t	o	r
w	a	o	e	d

2

c	u	o	u	y
s	l	n	n	d

3

s	o	e	n	t
r	w	u	e	d

4

r	t	u	g	h
s	o	o	n	e

5

p	r	u	n	h
b	a	i	s	t

1 ☐
2 ☐
3 ☐
4 ☐
5 ☐

Q. 6–10

missing letters

The same **two** letters end the first word and begin the next word. Write the letters.

Example T R A _I_ _L_   _I_ _L_ L N E S S

6   F R U __ __   __ __ E M

7   H I __ __   __ __ O S T

8   F I __ __   __ __ A T

9   R E __ __   __ __ J E C T I V E

10 J U I __ __   __ __ L E R Y

6 ☐
7 ☐
8 ☐
9 ☐
10 ☐

Q. 11–15

analogies

Underline **one** word in the brackets to complete these analogies.

Example Arrive is to depart as come is to (run hurry go hide).

11   Toe is to foot as finger is to (wrist elbow arm knuckle hand).

12   Sun is to day as moon is to (dusk night evening darkness stars).

13   Horn is to blow as harp is to (scrape fiddle bow music pluck).

14   Nose is to smell as eye is to (site hear sense see touch).

15   Two is to double as four is to (triple treble quadruple fourth quarter).

11 ☐
12 ☐
13 ☐
14 ☐
15 ☐

MARK ☐

MARK
✓ OR ✗

Q. 16–20

synonyms

Underline two words, **one** from **each** set of brackets, that are **similar** in meaning.

Example (large great <u>tiny</u> huge)   (box <u>small</u> hungry crate)

16	(hop drag catch down)	(throw press many pull)	16 ☐
17	(begin finish under serious)	(depart commence arrive slide)	17 ☐
18	(smart between relative friend)	(uncle relation dull below)	18 ☐
19	(loose shred below tight)	(under behind before begin)	19 ☐
20	(attempt descend forget stale)	(ascend fresh try conclude)	20 ☐

Q. 21–25

move a letter

Take **one** letter from the first word and put it in the second word to make two new words. Write the letter you have moved and the two new words in the table below.

	First word	Second word	Letter moved	New first word	New second word	
Example	slope	feat	s	lope	feast	
21	frail	hose				21 ☐
22	brain	pant				22 ☐
23	cause	gaze				23 ☐
24	ideal	fair				24 ☐
25	shame	tank				25 ☐

Q. 26–30

jumbled words with clues

Each question has a word in CAPITALS. The letters in this word have been mixed up. Use the clue to work out what the word is. Write it on the line.

Example NIBOR   (a bird)   <u>ROBIN</u>

26	CEROS (a football result)	_____	26 ☐
27	DRIBULE (puts up houses)	_____	27 ☐
28	CUFFILDIT (not easy)	_____	28 ☐
29	ELCLOCT (to gather together)	_____	29 ☐
30	HEARSP (a group of words)	_____	30 ☐

MARK ☐

MARK
✓ OR ✗

Q. 31–35

join two words to make one

Circle **one** word from **each** group which together will make a longer word.

Example (pond (dam) river)   (era down (age))

31	(mend break cure)	(ding ring fast)	31 ☐
32	(grit road tar)	(street get repairs)	32 ☐
33	(day evening morning)	(light bright early)	33 ☐
34	(traffic lamp stars)	(sign shine shade)	34 ☐
35	(pot jug cup)	(tea hole glare)	35 ☐

Q. 36–40

spot the word

A four-letter word is hidden in each of these sentences. You will find the hidden word at the end of one word and the beginning of the next. Underline the hidden word and then write it on the line.

Example Daniel <u>end</u>ed the speech with a joke.   <u> lend </u>

36   Go and ask in the post office where Derwent Road is. _____   36 ☐

37   We waited until the rain stopped before we began our journey.

   _____   37 ☐

38   I love reading stories about cowboys in the wild west. _____   38 ☐

39   You cannot play until everything in your room has been put away.

   _____   39 ☐

40   Mr Scott gave the pupils more advice on their career choices.

   _____   40 ☐

Q. 41–45

word categories

Underline the **general** word in each row, which is the word that includes all the others.

Example banana apple <u>fruit</u> raspberry pear kiwi

41	hyacinth flower tulip geranium rose marigold carnation	41 ☐
42	chisel hammer spanner saw tool pliers wrench mallet	42 ☐
43	weapon axe dagger sword pike lance spear	43 ☐
44	cotton nylon polyester fabric silk linen velvet	44 ☐
45	ebony mahogany pine walnut timber willow oak beech	45 ☐

MARK ☐

MARK
✓ OR ✗

Q. 46–50

true
statements

Read the information in each question. Circle the **only** statement (A, B, C, D or E) that has to be true, based on this information.

46 Manchester is north of Birmingham, which is north of Swindon. Swindon is north of Bournemouth, which overlooks the English Channel.
   A Swindon is north of Birmingham.
   B Manchester overlooks the English Channel.
   C Birmingham is south of Manchester.
   D Bournemouth is north of Swindon.
   E Swindon is south of Bournemouth.

46 ☐

47 Letters make up words. Words make up sentences. Sentences make up paragraphs. Words must be spelled correctly.
   A Words are made from letters.
   B Letters are made from paragraphs.
   C You need to be good at spelling.
   D Sentences are made from paper.
   E Paragraphs are made from books.

47 ☐

48 Eagles are birds. Eagles have wings and feathers. Eagles are predators. Baby eagles are called eaglets.
   A All eagles are eaglets.
   B Baby eagles lay eggs.
   C Eagles hunt.
   D All birds are eagles.
   E Eaglets are not eagles.

48 ☐

49 Grandpa is 80 years old. He has a daughter aged 50, who is my mother's sister.
   A My mother's sister is older than grandpa.
   B My mother's sister is my aunt.
   C Grandpa is younger than my mother.
   D Grandma is Grandpa's wife
   E My uncle is Grandpa's son.

49 ☐

50 Seven-year-old John is older than his sister Jen, who is three years younger. Jacob is three years older than his brother John and six years older than his sister.
   A Jen is the eldest child.
   B Jacob is ten years old.
   C Jen is eight years old.
   D John is older than Jacob.
   E John has two sisters.

50 ☐

MARK ☐

MARK
✓ OR ✗

Q. 51–55

word meanings

Each of these words can have **two** meanings. Write the numbers of the two meanings in the table below.

Example

		51		52		53		54		55	
organ		stable		rent		break		dart		shade	
11	12										

Meanings 1 to move quickly   2 to colour in   3 to damage something
4 out of the sun   5 money paid to live somewhere
6 a building for horses   7 a short rest from work
8 something sharp thrown at a board   9 steady and firm
10 ripped or torn   11 part of the body   12 a musical instrument

51 ☐
52 ☐
53 ☐
54 ☐
55 ☐

Q. 56–60

number sequences

Write the next two numbers in each sequence.

Example 2   4   6   8   <u>10</u>   <u>12</u>

56   7   9   13   19   27   _____   _____

57   14   11   21   18   28   25   35   _____   _____

58   3   7   13   21   31   _____   _____

59   31   29   32   30   33   _____   _____

60   87   73   59   45   31   _____   _____

56 ☐
57 ☐
58 ☐
59 ☐
60 ☐

Q. 61–65

letters for numbers

Find the answers to these calculations. Write each answer as a letter.

Example If C is 2, D is 8 and E is 10, answer this calculation. $C + D = $ ▢ <u>E</u>

61   If A is 4, B is 6, C is 8, D is 26 and E is 12, answer this calculation.

$B \times E \div A + C = $ ▢   _____

62   If A is 3, B is 15, C is 25, D is 75 and E is 5, answer this calculation.

$C \div E \times A = $ ▢   _____

63   If A is 8, B is 4, C is 2, D is 32 and E is 8, answer this calculation.

$A \times B \div C \div E = $ ▢   _____

64   If A is 5, B is 6, C is 9, and D is 8, answer this calculation.

$A + C - B = $ ▢   _____

65   If A is 4, B is 2, C is 10, D is 34 and E is 17, answer this calculation.

$D \div E + B = $ ▢   _____

61 ☐
62 ☐
63 ☐
64 ☐
65 ☐

MARK [   ]

MARK
✓ OR ✗

Q. 66–70

odd ones out

Two words in each question do **not** belong with the rest. Underline these **two** words.

Example horrid nasty <u>kind</u> mean unfriendly <u>helpful</u>

66	mystery	solution	puzzle	riddle	answer	66
67	famous	unknown	renowned	notable	obscure	67
68	uproar	silence	calm	noise	hullabaloo	68
69	fat	slender	obese	slim	stout	69
70	boundless	limitless	infinite	restricted	limited	70

Q. 71–75

complete the sentence

Underline **one** word in **each** set of brackets to make the sentence sensible.

Example The (plumber <u>electrician</u> baker) repaired the (<u>light</u> loaf sink) so that we could (lamp hear <u>see</u>) again.

71 The (dentist hedgehog sheriff) set out to arrest the (outlaw pigeon baker) and put him in (goal gaol custard). **71**

72 We always eat (cereal lollipops coffee) for our (burger birthday breakfast) before we go to (hospital school mushroom). **72**

73 My (aunt hamster uncle) is my (mother's son's grandfather's) (goldfish sister alien). **73**

74 The (pool pull swim) has (café water coffee) for (drinking washing swimming). **74**

75 A (hop leap skip) (day month year) happens every (two four ten) years. **75**

Q. 76–80

which word

One word in each question **can** be made from the word in CAPITALS. Underline this word. You may only use each letter once.

Example SPEEDBOAT toast debated poems <u>beast</u> poser

76	PRESENTATION	sentence	nation	resented	spread	feather	76
77	DESERVED	servant	drive	swerve	reseed	verdant	77
78	EPITOMISED	miser	misted	promise	polished	mister	78
79	DEFINITION	define	notion	noted	finish	tender	79
80	CHRONICLED	cornet	leader	rounded	deliver	circled	80

MARK

MARK
✓ OR ✗

Q. 81–85

alphabetical order

Number the words in each line in alphabetical order. Use the alphabet to help you.

Example HIGH   LOUD   TAKE   FAIL   MEAL
             2   3   5   1   4

A B C D E F G H I J K L M N O P Q R S T U V W X Y Z

81   TREE   MARBLE   COMB   DISTANCE   AMATEUR
      ☐   ☐   ☐   ☐   ☐   81 ☐

82   ORANGE   LEMON   PINEAPPLE   BANANA   FRUIT
      ☐   ☐   ☐   ☐   ☐   82 ☐

83   ONE   TWO   FOUR   SIX   EIGHT
      ☐   ☐   ☐   ☐   ☐   83 ☐

84   STICK   STOOL   STALE   STUPID   STEER
      ☐   ☐   ☐   ☐   ☐   84 ☐

85   GREEN   GREAT   GREMLIN   GREY   GRENADE
      ☐   ☐   ☐   ☐   ☐   85 ☐

Q. 86–90

missing three-letter words

In each of these sentences, the word in CAPITALS has three letters missing. These three letters make a real three-letter word. Write the three-letter word on the line.

Example My father SED me a photo of my mother.   _____HOW_____

86   My father's PNER is my mother.   _____   86 ☐

87   Our teacher took us to see and EXHIION of Dutch paintings.

                                                 _____   87 ☐

88   The HLE on the front door was broken.   _____   88 ☐

89   In autumn Ava loved to walk through the FEN leaves.

                                                 _____   89 ☐

90   The woman and her BEGROOM looked very happy.

                                                 _____   90 ☐

MARK ☐

MARK
✓ OR ✗

Q. 91–95
mixed-up groups

Two groups of three words have been mixed up in each question. Work out which would be the **middle** word in each group if they were in the correct order. Underline these **two** words.

Example city   <u>adolescent</u>   village   <u>town</u>   infant   adult

91	past	garden	field	future	moor	present	**91** ☐
92	tall	mound	mountain	short	medium	hill	**92** ☐
93	jack	exam	king	test	quiz	queen	**93** ☐
94	slice	greener	green	crumb	loaf	greenest	**94** ☐
95	duet	peckish	solo	starving	hungry	trio	**95** ☐

Q. 96–100
jumbled words in sentences

The letters of the words in CAPITALS have been mixed up. Write the **two** correct words on the lines.

Example The TERWA was too cold to WSIM in. <u>WATER</u> and <u>SWIM</u>

96 The RINAT passed through the station without PINGPOTS.

_____ and _____   **96** ☐

97 Our CODROT came to see Mum when she felt LUENWL.

_____ and _____   **97** ☐

98 Look both SWAY before crossing the DORA.

_____ and _____   **98** ☐

99 Jasmine came STRIF in the maths STET.

_____ and _____   **99** ☐

100 I am looking WARFORD to my summer LIDOHAY.

_____ and _____   **100** ☐

MARK ☐

END OF TEST

PAPER 5 TOTAL MARK ☐

Paper 6

MARK
✓ OR ✗

Q. 1–5

algebra

Work out these number problems. Write the answers on the lines.

1   If S = 5x + 2 and x = 10, what is S?   _____ | 1

2   If B = 3y − 8 and y = 25, what is B?   _____ | 2

3   If X = 3b + 5 and b = 8, what is X?   _____ | 3

4   If Z = 4a × 3 and a = 6, what is Z?   _____ | 4

5   If P = 7q ÷ 2 and q = 5, what is P?   _____ | 5

Q. 6–10

odd ones out

One word in each question does **not** belong with the rest. Underline this word.

Example horrid   nasty   kind   mean   unfriendly

6	ridiculous	amusing	funny	serious	hilarious	comical		6
7	fresh	new	modern	recent	up-to-date	ancient		7
8	reliable	faithful	dependable	true	devoted	untrustworthy		8
9	ghastly	horrible	beautiful	awful	dreadful	hideous		9
10	clear	obvious	plain	evident	hidden	apparent		10

Q. 11–15

word chains

Turn the word at the top of each grid into the word at the bottom. You can only change one letter at a time. Each change must result in a real word.

Example

T	A	L	E
T	A	K	E
L	A	K	E
L	I	K	E

11

D	A	L	E
M	O	R	E

12

B	Y	R	E
C	A	R	T

| 11 |
| 12 |

13

P	A	R	K
D	I	R	T

14

B	A	R	N
F	I	R	E

15

T	I	D	E
R	A	T	E

| 13 |
| 14 |
| 15 |

MARK [   ]

Schofield & Sims • Verbal Reasoning Progress Papers 1

MARK
✓ OR ✗

Q. 16–20

antonyms

Underline two words, **one** from **each** set of brackets, that have the **opposite** meaning.

Example (<u>happy</u>   kind   grin)   (<u>sad</u>   face   cheerful)

16	(melt water frozen)	(warm hot freeze)	16 ☐
17	(mate enemy friend)	(pal foe acquaintance)	17 ☐
18	(awake aware away)	(asphalt assert asleep)	18 ☐
19	(stern lenient leaning)	(strict cross punishment)	19 ☐
20	(pride prude proud)	(hurtful harmful humble)	20 ☐

Q. 21–25

position problems

Read the information carefully. Answer the questions.

21 Mark, Lucy, Majid, Thomas and Yasmin are 9, 10, 11, 12 and 13 years old, but not in that order. Two are older than Yasmin. Majid is the oldest. There are three younger than Thomas. Mark is not the youngest.

Who is the youngest in the group?   _____   21 ☐

22 Danek is taller than Preeti but not as tall as Maya, who is shorter than Amy.

Who is the tallest?   _____   22 ☐

23 A, B, C, D and E are people who live on the five floors of a block of flats. B can't climb stairs and can't use the lift. D presses floor 4 in the lift when going home. C lives midway between D and B. A has one flight of steps to climb. E does not like his neighbour upstairs.

What floor does A live on? Circle the correct answer.

ground floor   first floor   second floor   third floor   fourth floor   23 ☐

24 Joseph runs faster than Lily and Jai who are slower than Kim. Kim is not as fast as Joseph.

Who is the second fastest?   _____   24 ☐

25 In a group of five children, Chris is the tallest. Siraj is shorter than Chris but taller than Aaron and Jamie. Sophie is the only girl in the group and taller than three of the boys.

Who is the second tallest?   _____   25 ☐

MARK ☐

MARK
✓ OR ✗

Q. 26–30

symbol codes

The word **STAMEN** is written as ╬ ╟ ╚ ╗ ‖ ╡ in code. Use the same code to work out the hidden words.

26 ╗ ╚ ╡ ‖ ╬ _____ 26

27 ╡ ╚ ╗ ‖ ╬ _____ 27

28 ╡ ‖ ╚ ╟ _____ 28

29 ╗ ‖ ╚ ╡ ╬ _____ 29

30 ╬ ╟ ‖ ╚ ╗ _____ 30

Q. 31–35

letter sequences

Write the next two items in each sequence. Use the alphabet to help you.

Example AB CD EF GH <u>IJ</u> <u>KL</u>

A B C D E F G H I J K L M N O P Q R S T U V W X Y Z

31 AY   ZX   YW   XV   WU   VT   _____ _____ 31

32 BC   EF   HI   KL   NO   QR   _____ _____ 32

33 ER   GP   IN   KL   MJ   OH QF _____ _____ 33

34 BCE GHJ LMO QRT VWY _____ _____ 34

35 AX   EV   IT   MR   QP   UN   _____ _____ 35

Q. 36–40

spot the word

A four-letter word is hidden in each of these sentences. You will find the hidden word at the end of one word and the beginning of the next. Underline the hidden word and then write it on the line.

Example Daniel <u>end</u>ed the speech with a joke.   <u>lend</u>

36 Sometimes hunger can make your stomach rumble. _____ 36

37 Seth parked his car in the garage. _____ 37

38 Abbie fell and severely hurt herself. _____ 38

39 The beautiful lady posed for a photograph. _____ 39

40 The pupils went to learn French at lunchtime. _____ 40

MARK [ ]

MARK
✓ OR ✗

Q. 41–45

interpreting graphs

This graph shows the percentage of boys and girls who passed a maths test over a period of six years.

Study the graph. Then answer the questions.

The percentage of children who passed a maths test 2009 to 2014

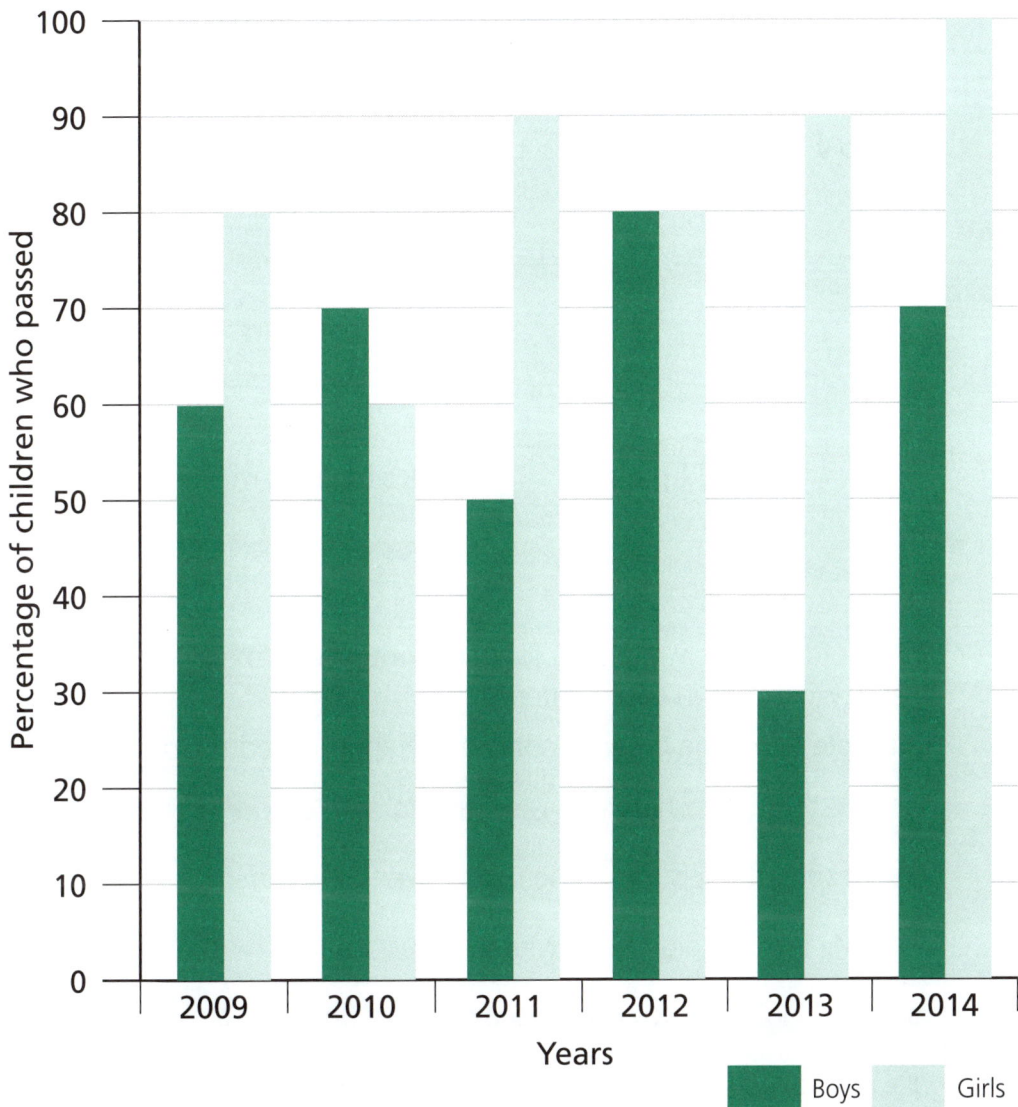

41 In which year did boys and girls have the same pass rate? _____ 41

42 In which year did the girls have three times as many passes as the boys?

_____ 42

43 Which was the only year when the boys did better than the girls?

_____ 43

44 Which was the worst year for the boys? _____ 44

45 Which was the best year of all for the girls? _____ 45

MARK

MARK
✓ OR ✗

Q. 46–50

jumbled words in grids

The letters at the bottom of each grid fit into the boxes above them to make **two** words. Work out where each letter goes.

46

v

r n a o v e e b

47

n

e o t n s i i h

48

p

s s p s r a t e

46 ☐

47 ☐

48 ☐

49

i

j l l l p a r t

50

e

k s l e a a c m

49 ☐

50 ☐

Q. 51–55

mixed-up sentences

Two words must swap places for each sentence to make sense. Underline these **two** words in each sentence.

Example The <u>bone</u> growled softly as he approached the <u>dog</u>.

51 Yesterday morning it was so raining hard on our way to school.

52 If something is mend then you have to broken it.

53 Me is much older than Mum.

54 As I looked down I could see the river flowing up the hill.

55 He looked on the chair and stood through the window.

51 ☐

52 ☐

53 ☐

54 ☐

55 ☐

Q. 56–60

word categories

Below this table are 10 words. Write each word in the correct column.

56 young	57 vegetables	58 fruit	59 birds	60 harness

canary   reins   kid   peach   eagle   pear
sprout   bridle   leek   calf

56 ☐

57 ☐

58 ☐

59 ☐

60 ☐

MARK ☐

MARK
✓ OR ✗

Q. 61–65

change a word

One word is incorrect in each sentence. Underline this word. Write the correct word on the line.

Example Climbing over that wall is not <u>aloud</u>.   <u>allowed</u>

61 Last week my sister Louise died her hair a different colour.

_____ | 61 ☐

62 The woman jumped from the plane and her parasol opened.

_____ | 62 ☐

63 My Aunt Rachel gave me a chum bracelet for my birthday.

_____ | 63 ☐

64 Dad asked the bank manger for a loan to buy the new car.

_____ | 64 ☐

65 This weekend James is going out to buy a new three piece suet.

_____ | 65 ☐

Q. 66–70

word connections

Underline the **one** word that fits with **both** pairs of words in brackets.

Example (heart club) (ruby emerald)   jewel brain <u>diamond</u> card brooch

66	(bandage strap) (throw hurl)	missile stone medicine sling plaster	66 ☐
67	(great good) (crushed ground)	excellent fine marvellous right	67 ☐
68	(dock harbour) (wine sherry)	seaside coffee lifeboat port drink	68 ☐
69	(final end) (persist stay)	result finish stop go last	69 ☐
70	(crimson green) (salt vinegar)	paint mustard condiment striped	70 ☐

Q. 71–75

number sequences

Write the next two numbers in each sequence.

Example 2 4 6 8 <u>10</u> <u>12</u>

71 7   8   10   13   17   22   28   ____ ____ | 71 ☐

72 1   9   7   16   13   23   ____ ____ | 72 ☐

73 15 17   21   27   35   45   ____ ____ | 73 ☐

74 2   6   4   8   6   10   8   ____ ____ | 74 ☐

75 13 26   16   32   22   44   ____ ____ | 75 ☐

MARK ☐

MARK
✓ OR ✗

Q. 76–80

analogies

Underline **one** word in the brackets to complete these analogies.

Example Arrive is to depart as come is to (run hurry <u>go</u> hide).

76 Triangle is to three as pentagon is to (four five six seven eight).   76 ☐

77 Bird is to nest as rabbit is to (field burrow stable house river).   77 ☐

78 Mobile is to telephone as tablet is to (pill computer handset medicine).   78 ☐

79 Water is to pipe as electricity is to (string box envelope wire shock).   79 ☐

80 Sole is to foot as palm is to (tree head arm wrist hand).   80 ☐

Q. 81–85

mixed-up
questions

The words are jumbled up in these questions. Work out what each question is. Then write the **answer** to that question. Put one letter in each box.

Example toes foot? are many How each on   ☐f☐ ☐i☐ ☐v☐ ☐e☐

81 is owl What a baby called?   ☐☐☐☐☐   81 ☐

82 called? brother What the a is of princess   ☐☐☐☐☐☐   82 ☐

83 is the on What we planet live called?   ☐☐☐☐☐   83 ☐

84 can we cow's What food milk? make from   ☐☐☐☐☐☐   84 ☐

85 barge a What sail does on?   ☐☐☐☐☐   85 ☐

Q. 86–90

which word

One word in each question **can** be made from the word in CAPITALS. Underline this word. You may only use each letter once.

Example SPEEDBOAT toast debated poems <u>beast</u> poser

86 OBSERVATION invite observe restore vacation servant   86 ☐

87 CONDIMENTS dimension comment stones mention count   87 ☐

88 DISENGAGED encourage greed singed gender danger   88 ☐

89 DELIGHTED lighten idled glittered tinge enlighten   89 ☐

90 PARLIAMENT means pleated entrails terminal trailer   90 ☐

MARK ☐

MARK
✓ OR ✗

Q. 91–95

add a letter

Read the clue in brackets. Add **one** letter to the word in CAPITALS to make a new word that matches the clue. Write the new word on the line.

Example CANE   (lifts heavy objects)   ___CRANE___

91	SENT (a pleasant smell)	_____	91 ☐
92	TOOT (used to bite and chew)	_____	92 ☐
93	OUGHT (purchased with money)	_____	93 ☐
94	CURT (a place where people face criminal charges)	_____	94 ☐
95	PLACE (the home of a king or queen)	_____	95 ☐

Q. 96–100

move a letter

Take **one** letter from the first word and put it in the second word to make two new words. Write the letter you have moved and the two new words in the table below.

	First word	Second word	Letter moved	New first word	New second word	
Example	slope	feat	s	lope	feast	
96	stare	tar				96 ☐
97	crimes	seas				97 ☐
98	table	right				98 ☐
99	raft	lint				99 ☐
100	trough	gave				100 ☐

MARK ☐

PAPER 6 TOTAL MARK ☐

END OF TEST

Progress chart

Write the score (out of 100) for each paper in the box provided at the bottom of the chart. Then colour in the column above the box to the appropriate height to represent this score.

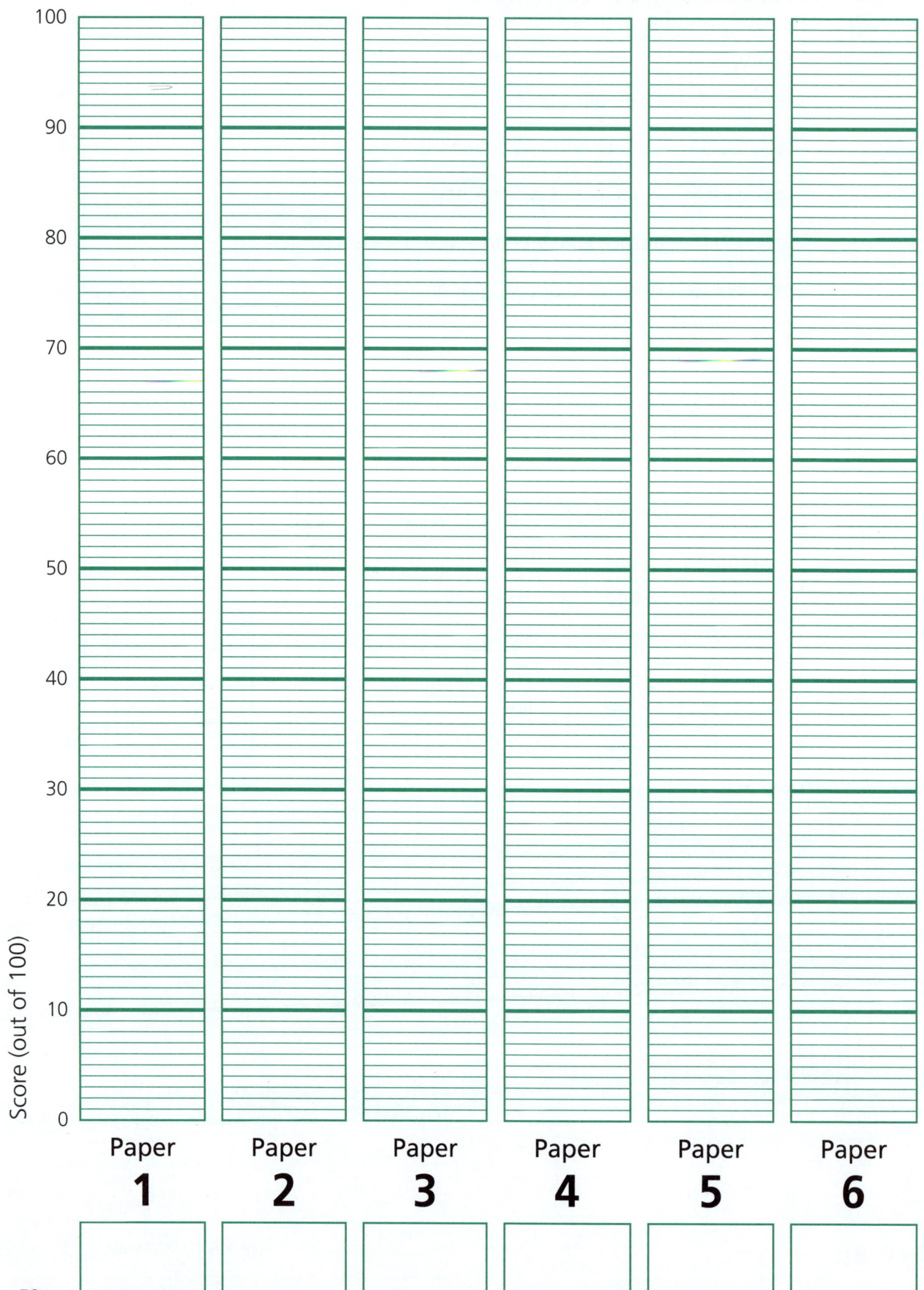

Score (out of 100)

100
90
80
70
60
50
40
30
20
10
0

Paper 1
Paper 2
Paper 3
Paper 4
Paper 5
Paper 6